The Alligator in the Closet

And Other Poems Around the House

The Alligator
in the Closet

And Other Poems Around the House

by David L. Harrison

illustrated by Jane Kendall

Wordsong
Boyds Mills Press

To Sandy,
always with love.
DLH

Text copyright © 2003 by David L. Harrison
Illustrations copyright © 2003 by Jane Kendall

Published by Wordsong
Boyds Mills Press, Inc.
A Highlights Company
815 Church Street
Honesdale, PA 18431
Printed in China

Publisher Cataloging-in-Publication Data (U.S)

Harrison, David Lee, 1937-
   The alligator in the closet : and other poems around the house /
by David L. Harrison ; illustrated by Jane Kendall. — 1st ed.
[48] p. : col. Ill. ; cm.
Summary: A collection of poems inspired by objects found around the house.
ISBN 1-56397-994-2
1. Home — Poetry — Juvenile literature. 2. Children's poetry, American.
[1. Home — Poetry. 2. American poetry.] I. Kendall, Jane. II. Title.
811/ .54   21   PS3558.A6657H68 2003
2002108453

First edition, 2003
Book designed by LDLDesigns
The text of this book is set in Bembo.
The illustrations are done in pen and ink and watercolor.

10 9 8 7 6 5 4 3 2 1

Table of Contents

The Guest in the Pantry

We have a pantry by the stair
And a mouse is living quietly there
In a clever nest he made himself
In a box of tissues on the shelf.

He seems to spend the day in bed,
His graceful tail around his head,
And never makes the slightest sound
To signify that he's around.

He's a gentlemanly mouse
In his house inside our house
And so we treat him as a guest
While he enjoys his daily rest.

He, in turn, is quite polite
To not disturb our sleep at night
While nibbling crumbs of this and that
With one eye on the napping cat.

He's not exactly like a pet —
Actually we've never met —
He's just the mouse beside the stair
And we don't mind him living there.

When You're Alone

A house makes noises
Of its own
Late at night
When you're alone.
Even though
No one is there,

Something creaks
Upon the stair,
Gurgles deep
Within the drain,

Scratches at
The windowpane,
Hisses sharply
Down the hall,

Pops its knuckles
In the wall,
Skitters quickly
On the roof

Until the dog
Lets out a woof
And kitty crawls
Into your lap.

No use hoping
You can nap.
Noises mutter
Crack and creep.
When you're alone,
Forget the sleep.

The Real Thing

Storybook crickets live in the hearth,
Ours lives under the bed,
Storybook crickets bring you luck,
We're losing sleep instead,
Storybook crickets sing and tap
With little umbrellas unfurled,
We'd better start hearing some storybook tunes
Or ours isn't long for this world.

Tock Talk *(for two voices)*

	TICK	TOCK
	TICK	TOCK
	TICK	TOCK
	TICK	TOCK
Clocks don't care!	TICK	TOCK
	TICK	TOCK
Clocks don't care	TICK	TOCK
If you toss all night!	TICK	TOCK
Clocks don't care!	TICK	TOCK
	TICK	TOCK
Clocks don't care	TICK	TOCK
If you don't sleep tight!	TICK	TOCK
All they ever do is	TICK	TOCK
	TICK	TOCK
All night through they	TICK	TOCK
	TICK	TOCK
Cover up your head they	TICK	TOCK
	TICK	TOCK
Roll around your bed they	TICK	TOCK
	TICK	TOCK
All night long they	TICK	TOCK
	TICK	TOCK
Same old song they	TICK	TOCK
	TICK	TOCK
Same old verse they	TICK	TOCK
	TICK	TOCK
What could be worse than	TICK	TOCK
	TICK	TOCK?

BRRRRINGGG!!!

The Dust Man

Resting on a dust ball
He snoozes through the day
Curled beneath the sofa
Or safely tucked away
Behind the dictionary
Or under the buffet
Until he hears you fall asleep
And knows it's time to play.

He dances on the mantel,
Brushes kitty's ball,
Tracks around the kitchen,
Scampers down the hall,
Scoots across the tables,
Touches every wall,
Paints the tops of picture frames
And ruffles on the doll.

He's quicker than a cricket
And lighter than the air,
No one's ever heard him
Creeping down the stair,
And no one's ever seen him
Slipping here and there,
But every night he leaves his work
Scattered everywhere.

On dusty feet he scurries
Grinning through the gloom,
Tosses tiny handfuls
Of dust in every room,
Bounces on the pillows,
Tiptoes by the broom,
And all the glass he saves for last,
Winking at the moon.

So wipe the coffee table
Till it sparkles in the light,
Polish all the china
Till there's not a speck in sight,
Clean the glass and mirrors
And rub with all your might,
He'll love it when there's work to do
While you're asleep tonight.

My Bed

Lazy me
Lazy day
I should be up
And on my way
Instead of lying
Here in bed
Pillows propped
Behind my head.

I should be dressed
But here I lie
Content to let
The world go by
Snuggled in
My toasty nest
Doing what
I love the best.

Lazy day
Lazy me
Nowhere else
I'd rather be
Than with a book
I haven't read
Cuddled down
To stay in bed!

Socks Without Partners

A sock without a partner
Is pretty hard to wear,
We have drawers of single socks
Without a single pair.

Wherever their mates are hiding
We wish they'd go there, too,
We paw through piles of single socks
And wonder what to do.

We would gladly toss them
But there's one important catch —
If their missing mates return
We wouldn't have a match.

This is a pressing problem
That no one should ignore —
We can't bear to throw them out
And every year there're more.

The Thermostat Wars
(for two voices)

No compromise on either side,
No one's ever satisfied,
Dad turns up the thermostat
And Mama turns it down.

In the frigid frosty winter
When snow blows all around
And sleet beats at the window
And rattles on the ground,
We quiver, shake, and shiver
And hope we won't be found
With the thermostat on 50,
In a lumpy frozen mound!

No compromise on either side,
No one's ever satisfied,
We always have the coldest
Or the hottest house in town.

So in the blazing summer
When blistering days return
And temperatures are boiling
We have a new concern —
We melt in sweaty puddles
Sizzling while we burn
With the thermostat on 90,
Wishing they would learn.

No compromise on either side,
No one's ever satisfied,
The battle of the thermostat
Rages up and down.

Keepers

Well sure it's true
They're not like new,
The soles have worn
A hole or two,

The shine is gone,
The leather's roughed,
The sides are cut,
The toes are scuffed,

One lace is missing,
One's in a knot,
I guess the heels
Don't look so hot,

But otherwise
They're hard to beat,
And I love the way
They fit my feet.

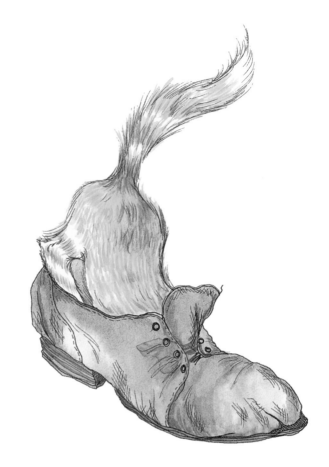

To the Victor

The victim lands
And slowly walks,
Silently the hunter stalks,
Edges closer —
Weapon high —
Will the hunted live or die?

Battle of wits,
Test of skill,
Matter of pride to make the kill.
The aim is true —
The effort grand —
But!
The fly is quicker than the hand.

Life's Not Fair!

I changed the roll
An hour ago
So there'd be plenty there.

I'm telling you
The roll was new,
We even had a spare.

So now I go,
And don't you know,
The roll's completely bare.

I have to yelp
And cry for help!
Life just isn't fair!

Family Heirlooms

Family heirlooms
Are a mystery!
Why would someone
In our history
Think they simply
Had to stop
To buy these vases
In some shop?

Are they worth a lot?
We hope!
Anybody like them?
Nope!
Are they works of beauty?
Yuck!
Why are they around?
We're stuck.

Someone passed them
Down to us
So they're not something
We discuss
Except to promise
When we're gone
We'll get revenge —
We'll pass them on!

My Chair

At times it's been a fortress,
A satellite in space,
A cavern full of dragons,
A secret hiding place,

A swamp for alligators,
A lookout in a tree,
A throne where I was ruler
As far as I could see.

Armies of my soldiers
Have fought beneath its feet,
The cushion's been an ocean
To sail my battle fleet.

It has held me for a sniffle
When things weren't going right,
And I've cuddled there for stories
Before I said good night.

Of all the things I count on
Nothing can compare
With sinking down in comfort
In my good old friendly chair.

Bad Guys

Need protection?
I'm your man!
I bark at bad guys
Loud as I can!
I've barked all day
Since I was a pup,
But how do they thank me?
"Hey! Shut up!"

I never rest
I watch the street
Through the window
On my feet
So when I see
A bad guy lurk
Grrr! I'm ready
To get to work!

I treat bad guys
All the same,
Protecting the family
Is my game,
I've barked all day
Since I was a pup,
And how do they thank me?

"Hey! Shut up!"

My Treasure

It's such a slender little book
Squeezed between a larger pair,
Unless you know just where to look
You could easily miss it there.

But it's worth more than all the host
Of books on shelves beside my bed.
I'll forever treasure most
This book—the first I ever read.

Who Was That?
I Don't Know!

(for two voices)

I love to look at photographs,
Especially ones from long ago,
To listen to the guessing games —

"Wasn't that old so-and-so?"

"You mean the guy in the funny hat?"
I Don't Know!

Who Was That?

*"Look at Paula's little girl!
I remember that old cat."*

"Who's the guy behind her dad?"

"Dressed up like a diplomat?"

"The tall one in the second row."

Who Was That?

I Don't Know!

Everybody takes a guess.

"There's Uncle Earl or Uncle Joe."

"Looks to me like Uncle Ned."

"Ned was always skinny though."

I Don't Know!

"So who's the guy who looks so fat?"

Who Was That?

"That's our cousin Donna Jean.
She was cute but what a brat!"

"I don't think that's Donna Jean.
Looks more like her sister Pat."

"Well, who's the one with the silly bow?"

Who Was That?

I Don't Know!

Whoever they were they're always there
With mischievous eyes and grins aglow
So I think we should give them names—

Who Was That

And *I Don't Know.*

Rolling in Butter

Through the window
Sunlight streams
To warm the kitty
Where she dreams

And interrupt
Her peaceful doze
With sunny kisses
On her nose.

Her yellow eyes
Like tiny suns
Regard the chance
To have some fun

She pounces on
The golden plot
Where sunlight paints
A buttery spot

And with a rumbly
Lazy purr
She rolls the sunlight
In her fur

And sleeps again
As easy as that,
A yellowy buttery
Rumbly cat.

Death of a Wasp

Bumping at the windowpane
He fought against the solid air
That held him as a prisoner there,
But all his struggles were in vain.

Never comprehending glass
Clear as air that stopped him hard
And blocked his freedom to the yard,
Repeatedly he tried to pass.

Eventually he lost his fight
And perished on a sunny sill
Facing toward his freedom still,
Wings awry in broken flight.

He had a name, Trypoxylon,
A small but vibrant living thing
Who came in by the door in spring
And in a day or two was gone.

The Alligator in the Closet
(for two voices)

Take this light and follow me.

What do you think we're going
to see?

Hard to say what there might be,
I think you'd better stick with me.

It sure is bigger than I thought.

It's full of things that I have caught,
Some are tame and some are not.

It holds a lot more than I thought!
So why do you keep the buffalo?

He has no other place to go,
He likes to roam in here and so
I have to keep the buffalo.

Holy cow! An alligator!

I used my aunt for bait.

He ate her?

With a little salt and tater.
I wouldn't pet the alligator.

Run for your life! A grizzly bear!

He loves to hibernate in there
Under piles of underwear.

I don't like your scary bear!
Let me out! I've seen enough!

Stay! We'll look for tamer stuff.
See my python? He's not rough.

But he might swallow me sure
eno…!

Under the Bed

Under the bed
It smells of must,
Socks and slippers,
Boxes, dust.

The sky's so low
It tickles your nose,
Your tummy mountain
Hides your toes.

Truth of it is
There's not much to it,
Except that no one else
Can do it.

Baby Spider

Noiselessly the spider plunges
Like a diver off my door,
A tiny living dot that dangles
Seven feet above the floor.

Bungee-jumping astronaut,
Miniature member of his race,
Letting out his silver cord
He works defenselessly in space.

Disappearing, reappearing,
Lost in shadow, bathed in light,
He slowly inches undetected,
Patient in his daring flight.

The floor at last beneath his feet
He ends his risky episode
And sets out on a new adventure
Down the carpet's nappy road.

Company's Coming!

What a mess!
A total wreck!
They're nearly here!
All hands on deck!

Clear the table!
Grab the shoes!
Make the beds!
No time to lose!

Cram the closets!
Slam the doors!
Hang the jackets!
Mop the floors!

Shove those socks
And underwear
And magazines
Beneath a chair!

Faster! Faster!
Not enough!
Move it! Shake it!
Hide this stuff!

Get some crackers
On a plate!
Pray that they
Are running late!

Slice the cheese!
Put out the cat!
Someone check
That thermostat!

Change the soap
And wipe the tile!
We're all sweaty!

Ding Dong!

Smile!

Baby Stuff

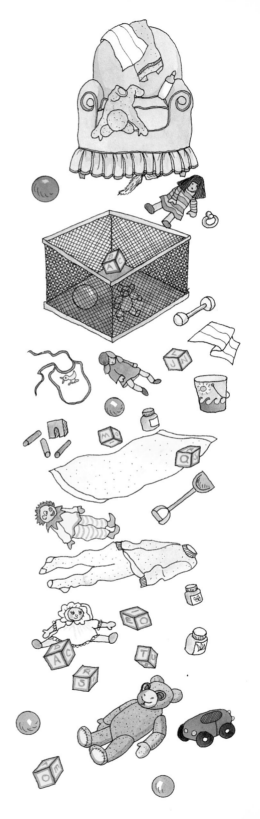

Diapers in the bathtub
Stroller in the hall
Highchair in the kitchen
Spinach on the wall
Drool on the tables
Crackers on the floor
Playpen by the sofa
Gate across the door
Cookies in the cushions
Bottles on the chairs
Teething rings and rattles
And ointment everywhere
Jars of yucky peaches
You wouldn't want to touch
Jammies, booties, blankets
A hundred times too much
Every seat is sticky
I recommend you stand
The baby stuff at our house
Is totally out of hand.

The Gift

Ugly
Ugly
Ugly
Clock!
Spindly arms!
Tinny tock!
Green ceramic!
Bulgy face!
Purple glass!
Pure disgrace!

This year's gift
From Uncle Ned!

Hide it!
Hide it
Under the bed
Beside the
Blue
Ceramic
Deer
We got
From Uncle Ned
Last year!

In Search of Jelly

Now and then
I yearn to spread
Some yummy jelly
On my bread,
But every jelly
Jar I find
Is full of something
Else instead.

Who knows what
The contents are?
This one looks
Like greenish tar,
This one says
It's made from grapes
But smells like something
Worse by far.

Here's some moldy
Barbecue,
Here's some gravy
Turned to glue,
This, I think,
Was bacon grease,
Here's a jar
Of fuzzy goo.

No matter how
I fuss and mutter
In search of jelly
In this clutter
There's nothing here
To spread on bread,
So once again,
It's peanut butter.

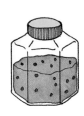

Under the Kitchen Table

There's a puppy under the table
Gazing up at me
With droopy tail and melty eyes
I cannot bear to see
And not hand down some tidbits
Whenever I am able
To sneak them past the grownups
Sitting at the table
Who act like feeding puppies
Is an awful sort of crime,
But droopy tail and melty eyes
Get me every time.

The Last Glass

In the beginning
There were eight
Graceful glasses
By our plates
For dinner parties,
Special guests,
Holidays,
And Sunday best.

Their elegance gave
A touch of class,
But time is hard
On fragile glass,
Cracks and chips
And hardwood floor
Reduced the set
From eight to four.

Still their number
Dwindled down
Till this last glass
Was left around
To gather dust
All by itself
Forgotten on
The cupboard shelf.

I love to use it
Now and then
And think of parties
Where it's been
For it was made
To grace a plate,
This one of a kind
From the elegant eight.

The Things We Do for Money

There's never an end
To the garbage and trash
I carry it out
There's more in a flash
Barrels and buckets
And oodles and gobs
Of whatchamacallits
And thingamabobs
From syrupy waffles
And buttery cobs
To slimy unspeakable
Glistening globs

It's gummy and gooey
And piled in a stack
I carry it out
And more grows back
Boxes and cartons
Of bottles and bags
A tottery tower
That teeters and sags

And threatens to fall
In a garbagy crash
There's never no never
Not ever an end
(But it beats doing dishes!)
To garbage and trash!

The Chili Bowl Story

This bowl came from a diner
In a village called Fair Play
Where people went for chili
When winter came to stay.

Bundled in their jackets,
Tracking in the snow,
They must have greeted neighbors
More than eighty years ago.

I bet they traded gossip
And talked of winter still
And lingered over chili
To cut the bitter chill.

Spoons would click and clatter
While people laughed away
Enjoying one another
On a cold and wintry day.

The diner's gone forever,
Shuttered up at last,
But when we use this chili bowl
I think about the past.

I think of all the stories
That we will never know
Of the hearty folk in Fair Play
A long long time ago.

Yard Sale

There's no place left
To put our stuff!
The house is full!
We have enough!
Stuff is piled
And boxed and stacked
Till every room's
Completely packed

With single earrings, birthday candles, bags of buttons,
scruffy sandals, half a dozen ballpoint pens, a bowling
ball, a contact lens, a fishing plug without a hook, a
book jacket without the book, a leaning lamp, a broken
chair, a one-armed tattered Teddy bear, turtle food,
a toilet seat, a cage to hold a parakeet, tomato stakes, a
roll of wire, half a hose, a tractor tire —

Sure it's junk
Without a doubt
But we would never
Throw it out
When there's a smarter
Thing to do —
Fill the yard
And sell it to you!

Home

The cat has clawed the furniture,
The dog has chewed the door,
The baby colored on the wall,
Chairs have scarred the floor.

The faucet in the shower leaks,
The table's full of stains,
The kitchen ceiling fills a pan
Every time it rains.

I guess it's not a perfect house,
As anyone can see,
But this is where my family is
So it's just right for me.